Giovanna Magi

PARIS

BONECHI

© Copyright 1992 by
CASA EDITRICE BONECHI
Via Cairoli 18/b
50131 Firenze
Telex 571323 CEB
Fax 55/5000766

Diffusion: OVET-PARIS
13, rue des Nanettes
75011 PARIS
Tel. 43.385.680

Printed in Italy by
Centro Stampa Editoriale Bonechi

ISBN 88-7009-006-X

CREDITS

Photos from the Archives of Casa Editrice Bonechi
taken by:
Gianni Dagli Orti: pages 11; 12; 13; 54; 56; 57.
Luigi Di Giovine: pages 50; 51; 55; 59 left.
Vincent Gauvreau: pages 38; 52; 53.
Paolo Giambone: pages 5; 6; 8 below; 9 below; 16
below; 17; 18; 19; 20; 21; 22; 23; 24; 25; 28; 29; 39;
41; 42; 43; 44; 45; 46; 47; 48; 49; 58; 59 right; 61.
Photo Gérard Boullay: pages 7; 8 above.
Jean Charles Pinheira: pages 9 above; 10; 27; 37;
40; 60; 62; 63.
© Photo Musées Nationaux: pages 30; 31; 32; 33;
34; 35; 47.

HISTORICAL NOTE

Writing a brief historical outline of Paris is no easy task: few cities have been so involved in great events which have changed the course of history. Its founders were probably the Gauls, who built a small settlement on the left bank of the Seine. The Romans reached here at an early stage, led by Julius Caesar, who in his " Gallic Wars " repeatedly mentions the town under the name of Lutetia. As a result of the continued and increasingly serious threat of the barbarian invasions, the original settlement was transferred to the island called Ile-de-la-Cité, from which point a slow but continuous expansion on both banks of the river began. The simple residence first of the Merovingian then of the Carolingian kings, Paris became a true capital in the year 987 when Ugo Capeto founded a new dynasty, raising the city to a status it was to retain throughout the entire course of the history of France. From this moment, Paris began to develop not only as an urban centre, but also from the cultural point of view. The accession to the throne of Philippe II Auguste, who reigned from 1180 to 1223, marked the beginning of one of Paris's most splendid periods: the construction of the Louvre was begun and in 1215 the University was founded. New splendour came with the reign of Louis IX (Louis the Blessed), which lasted from 1226 to 1270 and during which the Sainte-Chapelle was built and work on Nôtre-Dame considerably advanced. Under the following dynasty, that of the Valois, Paris experienced one of the most bitter periods in its history: 1358 was the year of the revolt headed by the leader of the Parisian merchants, Etienne Marcel. Charles V reestablished order, being responsible among other things for the construction of the Bastille, but the peace did not last. The civil war waged between the Armagnac and Burgundian factions permitted the occupation of France by England, Henry VI being crowned King of France in Nôtre-Dame in 1430. Finally, in 1437, Charles VII reconquered Paris but there were renewed internecine struggles and increasingly bloody revolts, alternating with terrible epidemics of the plague, which devastated the already distressed population. Then, throughout the 16th century, the importance of Paris was diminished in favour of the castles of the Loire, which the various kings who succeeded to the throne of France chose as their dwellings. This did nothing to put a halt to the internecine strife in the capital itself. The spread of the Protestant movement lay at the origin of the bloody religious struggles which for a long time rent Paris and France, culminating in the massacre of the Huguenots on 24 August 1572, the famous Night of St. Bartholomew. After the assassination of Henry III at St. Cloud by the young Jacques Clément in 1589, the city was besieged for four long years until it opened its gates to Henry IV, who had abandoned his original faith and been converted to Catholicism. All the same, at the beginning of the 17th century Paris already had a population of 300,000 persons. The city continued to grow in importance as a cultural and political centre, above all under the powerful Cardinal Richelieu, who in 1635 founded the Académie Française. During the new dynasty of the Bourbons, the city expanded even more: by 1715, during the reign of Louis XIV, it had half a million inhabitants. But Paris without doubt gained its place in history in 1789 with the beginning of the French Revolution, often seen as marking the birth of the modern world. Usually the Revolution is considered to have begun on 14 July of that year, when the people seized possession of that symbol of absolutism and terror, the prison of the Bastille. During the years which ensued, the historical developments came in ever more rapid succession: the monarchy fell, the Reign of Terror began, to be followed by the Thermidorian reaction, and in a short period of time the figures which had dominated the Parisian political scene disappeared for ever. What the city had suffered during those years (the loss of human life and the irreparable destruction of works of art) was forgotten with the advent of the Empire and the magnificent court which Napoleon created in 1804, when he was crowned in Nôtre-Dame by Pope Pius VII. From 1804 to 1814 the city was embellished with one artistic masterpiece after another: the column was erected in Place Vendôme, the Arch of Triumph was built and work continued on the Louvre, where in the luxurious Salon Carré in 1810 the marriage between Napoleon and Marie Louise of Austria was celebrated. Later again, Paris saw the fall of other monarchies, those of Charles X and Louis Philippe Bourbon-Orléans, and the birth of the Second Republic with the rise to the throne of Napoleon III. It was during the reign of the latter that Baron Haussman was given the task of replanning the city, thus solving

3

the difficult problem of traffic which was already choking the French capital. *The markets of Les Halles were constructed, the parks of the Bois de Boulogne and the Bois de Vincennes were designed, the Opéra was built and the main boulevards were reorganised.*

In 1870, the defeat suffered by Napoleon III at Sedan at the hands of the Prussians led to the revolt of the Parisians, which in turn initiated another unhappy moment in the history of the city, the period of the Commune (18 March-22 May 1871). Many beautiful and historic buildings were unfortunately destroyed in this period of rebellion, among others the splendid Hôtel de Ville and the Tuileries. *But at the beginning of the 20th century, Paris saw a new rise to splendour, with the World Fairs held there, the construction of the Grand Palais and the Petit Palais, and the birth of its new artistic movements, both in painting and in literature. Sad to say, the city had yet to suffer in two more long and bloody wars, which brought bombardments and ruins. In the second world war, it was taken by the German Army in 1940 and liberated by the Allies only in 1944. From that moment on, however, returning to its tradition as a free city full of life, Paris has retained its place in the history of mankind and its culture.*

NOTRE-DAME

Built on the site of a Christian basilica which had been occupied previously by a temple dating from Roman times, the church was begun in 1163 under Bishop Maurice de Sully, work commencing from the choir. As time passed the nave and aisles followed, and finally the façade was completed in about 1200 by Bishop Eudes de Sully, though the towers were not finished until 1245. The builders then turned to the construction of the chapels in the aisles and in the choir, under the direction of the architect Pierre de Chelles. In about 1250 another façade, that of the north arm of the transept, was completed, while the façade on the south arm was begun some eight years later. The church could be said to be finished in 1345. With the ravages of time and damages caused by men and by numerous tragic wars, the church's original appearance changed over the centuries, especially during the Revolution: in fact, in 1793 it ran the risk of being demolished. Nôtre-Dame at that point was dedicated to the Goddess of Reason, when Robespierre introduced this cult. But it was reconsecrated in 1802, in time for the pomp and ceremony of the coronation of Napoleon I by Pope Pius VII in 1804. After being threatened with destruction by fire in 1871, it underwent a definitive restoration by Viollet-le-Duc between 1844 and 1864. Imposing and majestic in its stylistic and formal consistency, the façade of Nôtre-Dame is divided vertically by pilasters into three parts and also divided horizontally by galleries into three sections, the lowest of which has three deep portals. Above this is the so-called Gallery of the Kings, with twenty-eight statues representing the kings of Israel and of Judaea. The Parisian people, who saw in them images of the hated French kings, pulled down the statues in 1793, but during the works of restoration at a later stage they were put back in their original place. The central section has two grandiose mullioned windows, on each side of the rose-window, which dates from 1220-1225 and is nearly 33 feet in diameter. This central section is also adorned by statues of the Madonna and Child and angels in the centre and of Adam and Eve at the sides. Above this runs a gallery of narrow, intertwined arch motifs, linking the two towers at the sides which were never completed but which, even without their spires, have a picturesque and fascinating quality with their tall mullioned windows. Here Viollet-le-Duc gave free rein to his imagination: he created an unreal world of demons who look down with ironic or pensive expressions on the distant city below, of birds with fantastic and imaginary forms, of the grotesque figures of leering monsters, emerging from the most disparate and unlikely points of the cathedral. Crouching on a Gothic pinnacle, half-hidden by a spire or hanging from the extension of a wall, these petrified figures seem to have been here for centuries, immobile, meditating on the destiny of the human race which swarms below them.

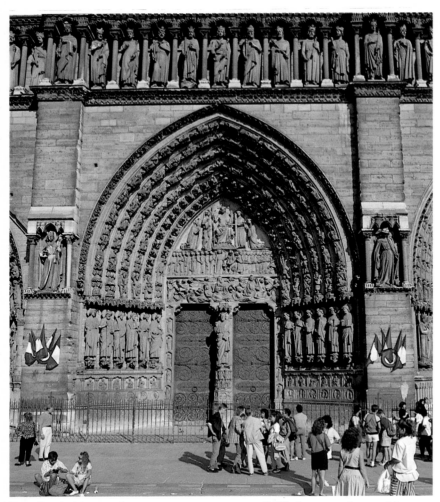

Detail of the portal

The Gothic style of these portals (dating from about 1220) is characterised by a softer and more direct way of looking at and interpreting nature, whereby the material is used to create more delicate forms and the space between one figure and another is more freely distributed. On the central portal is the subject perhaps best loved by the Gothic artists, that is, the Last Judgment. On the pilaster which divides it in two is the figure of Christ, while on the embrasures are panels with personifications of the vices and virtues and statues of the Apostles. Figures depicting the celestial court, Paradise and Hell are sculpted with great skill around the curve of the arch. The lunette with the Last Judgment is divided into three sections and is dominated by the figure of Christ, at whose sides are the Madonna, St. John and angels with symbols of the Passion. Beneath this on one side are the blessed who have merited salvation, and on the other side the damned being dragged towards their final punishment. In the lower strip is the Resurrection. The right-hand portal, called the Portal of St. Anne and built between 1160 and 1170, has reliefs dating from the 12th and 13th centuries, with a statue of St. Marcel, bishop of Paris in the 5th century, on the pilaster which divides it. In the lunette Our Lady is depicted between two angels and on the two sides are Bishop Maurice de Sully and King Louis VII. The third portal, the one on the left, is called the Portal of the Virgin and is perhaps the finest of the three because of its epic tone and the solemn grandeur of its sculpture. On the dividing pilaster is a Madonna and Child, a modern work. In the lunette above are the subjects dear to the iconography of the life of the Virgin, including her death, glorification and assumption. At the sides of the portal are figures depicting the months of the year, while in the embrasures are figures of saints and angels.

Interior

Entering the interior of the cathedral, one is immediately struck above all by its dimensions: no less than 426 feet long, 164 feet wide and 115 feet high, it can accommodate as many as 9000 persons. Cylindrical piers 16 feet in diameter divide the church into five aisles, and there is a double ambulatory around the transept and choir. A gallery with double openings runs around the apse above the arcades, being surmounted in turn by the ample windows from which a tranquil light enters the church. Chapels rich in art-works from the 17th and 18th centuries line the aisles up to the transverse arm of the transept. At each end of the transept are rose-windows containing splendid stained-glass pieces dating from the 11th century; particularly outstanding is the stained-glass window of the north arm, dating from about 1250, with scenes from the Old Testament and a Madonna and Child in the centre, justly celebrated for the marvellous blue tones which it radiates. From the transept one passes into the choir, at the entrance to which are two piers; the pier on the north has the famous statue of Nôtre-Dame-de-Paris, dating from the 14th century and brought here from the Chapel of St. Aignan. An 18th-century carved wooden choir surrounds half of the presbytery, and on the high altar is a statue of the Pietà by Nicolas Coustou; at the sides of this are two more statues, one representing Louis XIII by Giullaume Cousteau and the other Louis XIV by Coysevox. Finally there is the ambulatory with radial chapels which contain numerous tombs. On the right, between the Chapelle Saint-Denis and the Chapelle Sainte-Madeleine, is the en-

trance to the Treasury, in which can be seen relics and sacred silverware. Among the most important relics are a fragment of the True Cross, the Crown of Thorns and the Sacred Nail. At this point, having reached the end of the church, if one turns towards the main entrance one cannot help being struck by the great rose-window above the 18th-century organ, in which are depicted the signs of the zodiac with images of the months and of the vices and virtues.

Interior: south rose-window

A work of the 13th century, but restored in the 18th century, it depicts Christ in the act of benediction surrounded by apostles and the wise virgins and foolish virgins. The richness and luminosity of the colours and the precise placing of the glass tesserae combine to give almost the impression that a single, intensely bright star is bursting, throwing its splendid rays of light in every direction.

Apse

From the bridge called Pont de la Tournelle, constructed in 1370 but rebuilt many times, one can see the vast curve of the apse of Nôtre-Dame. In other churches, the part centring on the apse usually aims at gathering together, as if in an embrace, all the lines of force and the rhythmic and spatial values of the interior. But here the apse creates its own rhythm, serving as a terminal point but also creating a new sense of movement which extends to every structural element, from the rampant arches to the ribbing. The rampant arches, which here reach a radius of nearly 50 feet, are the work of Jean Ravy.

Right side of the Cathedral

An evocative view of the right side of the cathedral can be had from the colourful quay of Montebello, one of those streets along the Seine always so full of animated life. The " bouquinistes ", the famous sellers of prints old and new where rare and curious books can also be found, give this street its peculiar flavour and typical Parisian spirit.

LA CONCIERGERIE

This severe and imposing building on the banks of the Seine dates from the time of Philip the Fair, that is between the end of the 13th and the beginning of the 14th centuries. Its name derives from " concierge ", name of the royal governor who was in charge of the building. Today it constitutes a wing of the Palais de Justice. A visit to the castle is of considerable interest, since it is full of memories and takes the visitor back to distant and troubled times of conspiracy and revolution. In fact, from the 16th century on it served as a state prison. Then, during the Revolution, its cells were occupied by thousands of citizens who lived out their last hours here before climbing the steps to the guillotine. On the ground floor is the Hall of the Guards, with power-ful piers supporting Gothic vaults, and the large Hall of the Men-at-Arms. The latter room, which has four aisles and is no less than 224 feet long, 88 feet wide and 26 feet high, was once the dining-hall of the king. From the nearby kitchens the expert cooks of the royal house were capable of preparing meals for at least a thousand guests. To speak of the Conciergerie, however, takes us above all back to the time of the Revolution; visiting the cells and learning the segrets of the building we are following the last footsteps of those condemned to death, many of whose names are only too well known. In a large room on the ground floor, with cruciform vaults, the prisoners could have, for a certain fee, a straw pallet on which to sleep; in another area, with the tragically ironic name of Rue de Paris, the poor prisoners were quartered. The cell of Marie Antoinette, convert-ed into a chapel in 1816 by the only remaining daughter of Louis XVI, the Duchess of Angoulême, is perhaps the most evocative of all: here the royal prisoner, scornfully called the " Austrian woman ", lived from 2 August 1793 until 16 October; on this Wednesday morn-ing, at 7 o'clock, after cutting her own hair, she too climbed on the cart to be taken to the scaffold where nine months before her hus-band had died.

SAINTE CHAPELLE

From the courtyard of the Palais de Justice, through a vaulted pas-sageway, one reaches that master-piece of Gothic architecture which is the Sainte Chapelle. It was built for Louis IX (Louis the Blessed) to contain the relic of the crown of thorns which the king had bought

in Venice in 1239; the relic had been brought to Venice from Constantinople. The architect who planned the chapel was probably Pierre de Montreuil, the architect of Saint Germain des Prés; here he actually designed two chapels, standing one above the other, and they were consecrated in 1248. The lower church acts as a high base for the overall structure, above it being large windows crowned with cusps. The steep sloping roof is adorned by a slim and delicate marble balustrade, and this graceful piece of architecture is splendidly crowned by a slender openwork spire 246 feet high. Two more towers with spires stand on each side of the façade, in front of which is a porch; above the porch is a

large rose-window with cusps, dating from the end of the 15th century, its subject illustrating the Apocalypse. The whole work is marked by its lightness: the structural elements lose their consistency to become subtle embroidery, delicate lacework. The ribbing becomes slender, the pinnacles finer, until the architecture almost disappears, leaving only the huge stained-glass windows.

SAINTE CHAPELLE
Lower Church

There is without doubt a sudden change of atmosphere, style and emotion when one descends from the Upper to the Lower Chapel.

Only 23 feet high, it has three aisles, but the nave is enormous compared to the two much smaller aisles at the sides. Trilobate arch motifs supported by shafts recur along the walls. The apse at the end is polygonal. But here too, as in the Upper Chapel, it is the colour which predominates. The rich polychrome decoration overshadows the architecture, which is thus transformed into a simple support for the decorative element.

SAINTE CHAPELLE
Upper Church

Climbing a staircase from the Lower Chapel, one reaches the Upper Chapel, a splendid reliquary

with the appearance of a precious jewel-case. Without aisles, it is 55 feet wide and 67 feet high. A high plinth runs all around the church, interrupted by perforated marble arcades which from time to time open up onto deep niches. In the third bay are the two niches reserved for the king and his family. On each pillar is a 14th-century statue of an Apostle. The architecture is thus lightened as much as possible in order to leave room for the huge stained-glass windows, nearly 50 feet high. Whereas in the art of the Romanesque period a church's paintings had been half-hidden in an apse, in the curve of an arch or under a wide vault, here in this Gothic creation the pictures are magnificently transferred to the stained-glass windows, triumphantly presented to the gaze of all and illuminating the whole church with their precious colours. The fifteen stained-glass windows of the Sainte Chapelle, belonging to the 13th century, contain 1134 scenes and cover an area of 6650 square feet; they illustrate, in splendid colours and in an excited, almost feverish style, Biblical and Evangelical scenes.

PONT NEUF

Despite its name, which means "New Bridge", the Pont Neuf, designed by Du Cerceau and Des Illes, is the oldest bridge in Paris: it was begun in 1578 under Henry III and completed under Henry IV in 1606. From the point of view of its design, however, it is decidedly a "new" bridge, indeed revolutionary compared with previous designs. All the other bridges in the city, in fact, had had tall houses built on the sides, hiding the view of the river. Here instead a perspective on the Seine was created and the bridge, with its two round arches, became an enormous balcony thrust out over the river. The Parisians appreciated its beauty and importance at once, and the bridge became a meeting place and favourite promenade. At the beginning of the 17th century, it even saw the birth of the French comic theatre, when the famous Tabarin gave his performances here.

HÔTEL DE VILLE

In the centre of a huge square which for five centuries was the site of public executions is the venerable Hôtel de Ville, today the municipal headquarters of the city. On the site which it occupies there was previously a 16th-century building, designed by Domenico da Cortona: built in the Renaissance style, it was destroyed by fire in 1871, during the struggles which led to the fall of the Commune. The later building thus takes its inspiration from this lost edifice. It was designed by the architects Deperthes and Ballu, who completed it in 1882. The complex is certainly imposing and original, with its various pavilions surmounted by domes in the shape of truncated pyramids and with a forest of statues in every angle. In fact, there are no less than 136 statues on the four façades of the building, while on the terrace is the statue depicting Etienne Marcel, leader of the Parisian marchants and fomenter of the disorders which crippled Paris in the 14th century. Over the centuries the building has been the scene of important historical events. The most tragic of all, perhaps, took place on the morning of 27 July 1794, the day which in the new calendar created by the Republicans was called the 9th of Thermidor. Robespierre, the Incorruptible, was closed inside the Hôtel with his followers, trying to find a way of avoiding the threat of a civil war which he knew would certainly create havoc among the factions that had emerged within the Republican system. When the soldiers of the Convention burst into the room, Robespierre tried to commit suicide by shooting himself in the throat, but he succeeded only in inflicting a jaw wound. He was dragged off, to be executed the following day.

TOUR SAINT JACQUES

Erected between 1508 and 1522, it is 170 feet high and belongs to the most elaborate Gothic style. Narrow windows alternate with niches crowned by spires and pinnacles, in which there are many statues. The statue at the top of the tower of St. James the Greater is by Chenillon (1870).

PLACE DES VICTOIRES

This square, circular in form, came into being in 1685 as a surrounding for the allegorical statue of Louis XIV, commissioned from Desjardins by the Duke de la Feuillade. The statue, destroyed during the Revolution in 1792, was replaced in 1822 with another in bronze by Bosio.

PLACE DU CHÂTELET

The square takes its name from the ancient fortress, the Grand Châtelet, built to defend the Pont au Change in front of it and destroyed under Napoleon I. But the present appearance of the square dates from the time of Napoleon III. In the centre is the Châtelet Fountain (also called the Fountain of Victory or of the Palm), with its base adorned by sphinxes and statues, dating from 1858.

POMPIDOU CENTRE (Beaubourg)

In 1969, the then President of the Republic, Georges Pompidou, decided to create an important cultural centre in the area known as the "plateau Beaubourg". An international call to tender was announced and the project of Renzo Piano and Richard Rogers was accepted. Building began in April 1972 and the centre was opened by Giscard d'Estaing on the 31st January 1977. The building, an "urban machine", as it has often been described, occupies an area of one hundred metres square. Each external pipeline is painted a different colour because each colour corresponds to a different function: blue corresponds to the climatization plant, jellow the electrical installation, red the circulation and green the water circuits. The **National Museum of Modern Art** occupies the top three floors of the Pompidou Centre. Near the Beaubourg, the original, colourful and amusing *fountain by Tinguely*, the kinetic sculptor belonging to the Nouveau Réalisme group, officially formed in Paris on the 27th October 1960.

FORUM DES HALLES

Les Halles, the oldest district of Paris, is also the liveliest and most vivacious. Emilie Zola once described it, with a colourful expression, as the "belly of Paris": in fact, the city wholesale grocery market once stood here: ten pavilions of iron, steel and cast iron, transferred to Rungis in March 1969.
At the feet of the Gothic Church of St Eustache, within a new concept of urban space, rose the Forum, over forty thousand square metres of glass and aluminium, marble stairways and furniture, developped over four underground levels and around a quadrangular open-air square. Inaugurated on 4th September 1979 and based on a project by two architects, Claude Vasconi and Georges Pencreac'h, it can truly be said that the Forum has everything: shops for clothes, objets d'art and gastronomy, everything for the house, places of entertainment, restaurants and ten cinemas, banks and information centres. There are also four lines of the métro and two lines of the RER.

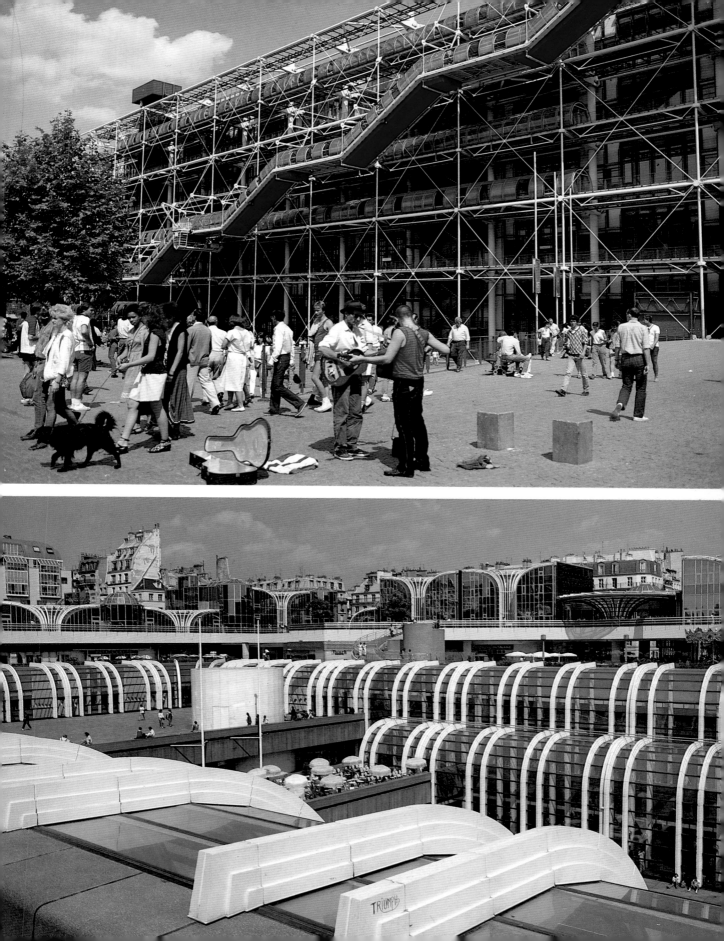

MOLIERE'S HOUSE

Two houses bear witness to Molière's life in Paris. He was born in 1622 in the house at No. 21 Rue Saint-Honoré. Having fallen ill on the stage of the Palais Royal on 17th February 1673, he was transported, dying, to the house at No. 40 Rue de Richelieu.

LE QUARTIER DE L'HORLOGE

Alongside Pompidou Centre, this modern pedestrian district owes its name to Jacques Monestier's famous clock, installed in 1979. Built of brass and steel, this device is electronically driven and programmed. At the chime of every hour, an automaton armed with a sword and shield combats and defeats the three animals surrounding it, symbolizing the three elements: Dragon-Earth, Bird-Air and Crab-Water.

THE PRODUCE EXCHANGE
(Bourse du Commerce)

The old wheat market built in 1765 by the provost of the traders, the Produce Exchange is nowadays an imposing circular building adorned with a monumental series of paired pilaster strips. The offices form a crown around the large inner hall topped by a dome in glass and steel.

SAINT-EUSTACHE

At the edge of the area once occupied by the central food market, Saint-Eustache is one of the most surprising churches in Paris. Building commenced in 1532 and ended only in 1637. It is distinguished by an unusual mixture of styles: a plan based on that of Notre-Dame, flamboyant Gothic vaults and Renaissance decoration consisting of three rows of superposed, tapered columns.
In a chapel of the choir lies the tomb of Colbert, Louis XIV's famous finance minister, by the sculptors Coysevox and Tuby according to a drawing by Le Brun.

PALAIS ROYAL

This palace, built by Lemercier between 1624 and 1645, was originally the private residence of Cardinal Richelieu, who bequeathed it on his death in 1642 to Louis XIII. Today the seat of the Council of State, it has a colonnaded façade erected in 1774 and a small courtyard, from which one passes through a double colonnade into its beautiful and famous garden. The garden, planned in 1781 by Louis, extends for nearly 250 yards, with green elms and lime-trees and a profusion of statues. It is surrounded on three sides by robust pillars and a portico which today accommodates interesting shops with antiques and rare books. During the Revolution it became a meeting-place for patriots: here the anti-monarchist aristocrats, among them the Duke of Orléans who was later to be rebaptised Philippe Egalité, met to discuss the state of the country and the historical developments about to be unleashed. In these gardens, in front of the Café Foy to be exact, on 12 July 1789, Camille Desmoulins harangued the crowd, inflaming them with his passionate speech. Later, he was to tear a green leaf from one of these trees and put it in his hat as a cockade. The crowd followed his example and two days later, at the storming of the Bastille, many wore the leaf emblem.

PLACE DES PYRAMIDES

Along Rue de Rivoli, almost at the level of the Pavillon de Marsan, is the small, rectangular square called Place des Pyramides, which has buildings with porticoes on three sides. In the centre of the square is the equestrian statue of Joan of Arc, a work done by Frémiet in 1874 which attracts pilgrimages every year.

ST. GERMAIN L'AUXERROIS

In front of the eastern part of the Louvre is a small square dominated by the symmetrical façades of the Mairie, or town-hall, of Paris's First Arrondissement, dating from 1859, and of the church of St. Germain l'Auxerrois. The two buildings are separated by a bell-tower, built in the neo-Gothic style in 1860. Also called the "Grande Paroisse", the Great Parish Church, because it was the royal chapel of the Louvre in the 14th century, St. Germain l'Auxerrois stands on the site of a previous sanctuary dating from the Merovingian era. Its construction was begun in the 12th century and continued until the 16th. On the façade is a deep porch built between 1435 and 1439 in the Gothic style, with five arches, each one different from the others, its pillars adorned by statues. Other statues, depicting saints and kings, are in the three portals. Higher up is a fine rose-window surmounted by a cusp, next to which is the church's bell-tower dating from the 11th century. The sight of the interior of the church is impressive: it has five aisles, divided by piers, transept and choir. It also contains numerous works of art, among which a worthy example is the royal pew which F. Mercier carved from wood in 1682. Also in polychrome wood is the statue depicting St. Germain, while the statue of St. Vincent is of stone but it too is enlivened by the use of warm colours. Both these works date from the 15th century. Among other works of art worth mentioning is a Flemish reredos in carved wood, the scenes of which depict moments in the life of Jesus.

RUE DE RIVOLI

This street, parallel to the Seine, connects Place de la Concorde to Place de la Bastille. It is one of Napoleon's greatest urbanistic successes – by two architects of the empire, Percier and Fontaine – but it was only completed during the reign of Louis-Philippe. In the section that skirts the Tuileries and the Louvre, one can admire, on the one side, an elegant portico with numerous clothing and souvenir stores.

THE LOUVRE

History of the palace and museum

The origin of the Louvre dates back to the 13th century, when Philippe Auguste had a fortress built near the river for defensive purposes: the fortress occupied about a quarter of what is now the Cour Carrée, or Square Courtyard. Not yet a royal dwelling (in fact the king preferred to live on the Ile de la Cité), the fortress contained within its sturdy walls the royal treasury and archives. In the 14th century, Charles -V, known as Charles the Wise, made the building more inhabitable and converted it into his royal residence; among other things he ordered the construction of the famous Librairie, meriting for this work alone the historic appellative by which he is known. After his reign, however, the Louvre was not to be used as a royal palace until 1546, when Francis I commissioned the architect Pierre Lescot to carry out alterations and extensions which would adapt it more to the tastes of the Renaissance. To do so, Lescot had the old fortress demolished and the new palace erected on its foundations. Work continued under Henry II, still under the direction of Lescot who, for the sculpture, had the collaboration of Jean Goujon. After the death in a tournament of Henry II, his widow, Caterina de' Medici, entrusted Philibert Delorme with the task of constructing the Tuileries Palace and uniting it to the Louvre by means of a long wing which extended towards the Seine. Work was interrupted on the death of Delorme, but resumed and completed under Henry IV, who had the Pavillon de Flore built. The building was further enlarged under Louis XIII and Louis XIV, with the completion of the Cour Carrée, which because of the wealth of its sculptural decorations became the most distinguished part of the so-called Old Louvre, and the building of the east façade with the colonnade. When the royal court was transferred to Versailles in 1682, work was virtually abandoned and the Louvre fell into such a state of ruin that in 1750 its demolition was even considered. It could be said that the women of the Parisian markets saved the building when, with their march on Versailles on 6 October 1789, they forced the royal family to return to Paris. After the tormented years of the Revolution, work on the building was eventually resumed by Napoleon, whose architects Percier and Fontaine began the construction of the north wing, finished in 1852 by Napoleon III, who finally decided to complete the Louvre. After the fire which destroyed the Tuileries in May 1871, the Louvre assumed the appearance which it still has today.

Following the dispersion of the important Librairie of Charles the Wise, it was Francis I in the 16th century who began a collection of art works, the first nucleus of what was to become one of the most important collections in the world. This was considerably enlarged under Louis XIII and Louis XIV, and indeed by the time the latter died the Louvre was regularly the scene of exhibitions of painting and sculpture. Finally, on 10 August 1793, the gallery was opened to the public and thus became a museum. From then on, the collection was continuously enlarged, not least by Napoleon I who demanded a tribute in works of art from the nations he conquered. The objects contained in the museum's catalogue today amount to about 400,000, subdivided into their various sections which range from ancient Egyptian, Greek and Roman works to those from the Orient, from medieval to modern sculpture, and objets d'art such as those belonging to the Royal Treasury to the immense collections of paintings.

"Le Grand Louvre" - This is the *"Grand Louvre" after the recent restructuring work.*
The project took off in 1981 with the decision by the President of the Republic, Mitterrand, to return the building to its original function, that of a Museum. First of all the Exchequer, which occupied the Flora Pavilion, was transferred to Bercy. The trait-d'union between the new rooms and the surface is a glass, transparent pyramid flanked by another two smaller pyramids. The author of this bold project was the American architect of Chinese origin, Ieoh Ming Pei.

The Colonnade

Before this colonnade was built, the minister at the time, Colbert, summoned Bernini from Rome, and in 1665 the great Italian artist presented a plan which was clearly Baroque in flavour. Since this did not correspond to the tastes of the French court, which was already inclining towards neo-classical forms in which a reverence for the ancient world and an academic culture could be felt, the project was then entrusted to Claude Perrault, who between 1667 and 1673 directed the erection of this famous monumental colonnade. Made up of extremely tall twin columns, for which Perrault used iron reinforcement, the long gallery runs along a high base, interrupted by windows. Three architectural masses, of which the central one is crowned by a pediment, project from the façade. The motif of two opposing L's, surrounded by garlands within a medallion, which recurs along the façade, is the seal of Louis XIV.

following page:
Square Courtyard and Clock Pavilion

This grandiose courtyard, more than 390 feet long on each side, was originally the enclosure in the early castle built by Philippe Auguste. The buildings here reveal various phases of construction, but the most interesting part is without doubt the central pavilion, built by Pierre Lescot and consisting of two orders of windows surmounted by an attic. The whole façade of this wing was also richly decorated with statues and reliefs by Jean Goujon and his school. In the centre of the wing is the Clock Pavilion, designed by Lemercier under Louis XIII; its construction, begun in 1624, was made possible by the demolition of the " Librairie " Tower, part of the Louvre as it was at the time of Charles V. At a later time, during the Restoration, the clock visible today was erected in place of a previous window, while the sculptors Buyster, Poissant and Guérin were responsible for the powerful caryatids standing below the cupola. Louis le Vau designed the other three wings of the courtyard, which originally had two floors though these were later increased to three by Percier and Fontaine, the architects of Napoleon I.

Venus de Milo

Discovered in 1820 by a peasant
on the island of Milo in the Cyc-
lades, this statue has come to be
considered the prototype of Greek
feminine beauty. Somewhat more
than 6 feet high, with its arms
broken off (no one has ever succeeded in establishing what the
original position of the arms was),
it belongs to the Hellenistic Age,
that is to the end of the 2nd century B.C., but it almost certainly
derives from an original by Prax-
iteles. Like the other works by this
great sculptor, the figure is slightly
off balance, as if resting on an
imaginary support, which gives a
delicate curve and twisting movement to the bust. Critics and art
lovers have long gazed on the
slender nude body of the goddess
emerging from the heavy cloth of
her cloak which is slipping towards
the ground. The material of the
statue itself, Parian marble, gives
the goddess's body and skin a
lightness worthy of the finest
classical traditions.

Hellenistic Art
Nike of Samothrace

Found in 1863 at Samothrace, with
the head and arms missing (one
hand was discovered in 1950), this
work dates from about 190 B.C.,
a period when the inhabitants of
Rhodes had a series of military
victories against Antioch III. The
Nike (or Victory figure) stands erect
on the prow of the ship which she
will guide to victory: the sea wind
hits her with all its force, tearing at
her clothing and pressing it to her
body. The clothing here is treated
in an almost Baroque way (which
would fully justify the rather late
date assigned to the work): it vi-
brates in contact with the Victory's
body and flaps in the wind, which
in turn pushes the Victory's arms
violently backwards. About 9 feet
high and made from Parian marble,
this is without doubt one of the
most important works of the entire
range of Hellenistic statuary.

*Eugene Delacroix
(1798-1863)*
Death of Sardanapalos

Exhibited in the Salon in 1827-1828, this canvas was little appreciated because of its errors in perspective and above all because of the confusion which reigns in the foreground. The catologue of the Salon describes it thus: " .... the insurgents besiege him in his palace.... Reclining on a splendid bed, at the top of a huge pyre, Sardanapalos orders the eunuchs and servants of the royal palace to butcher the women and pages and even his favourite horses and dogs.... Aisheh, the Bactrian woman, because she cannot endure to be put to death by a slave, hangs herself from the columns which support the vault.... ". But Delacroix was not seeking order and precision of detail: his intention was to upset, disturb and exalt the mind of the viewer. The fascination of the Orient, the artist's long stay in Spain and Morocco and his celebration of the exotic and the mysterious have all left their mark on this canvas, as for example in the brilliant colours and in the gleam of the gold which blends with the red of the fabrics. Standing out above all is the sovereign, with his closed, indifferent expression, as he watches, unmoved by the massacre.

Jacques-Louis David (1748-1825)
Coronation of Napoleon I

With the coming of the French Revolution and the great changes which it brought in every field, artistic canons too were overturned. Rococo elegance was banished, and it was the Academy with its official tastes which now dictated the rules. The new era required its own interpreter and found him in Jacques-Louis David, who had been in sympathy with the revolutionaries and now became a fervent admirer of Napoleon, at whose side and under whose patronage he worked with great energy. After numerous sketches and drawings, David painted this enormous canvas with a surface of 580 square feet, representing the coronation of Napoleon which took place on 2 December 1804 in Nôtre-Dame. David worked on it from 1805 to 1807, with the help of his pupil Rouget as well, painting no less than 150 portraits, all of them vivid and solemn images. This work, which confirmed David definitively as the most important painter of the new Empire, displays an outstanding sense of equilibrium in its composition, besides solemnity and nobility of expression. One might say that each image and each figure (all historically recognisable) constitutes a portrait in itself because of the accuracy with which they are conceived and the coherency with which they are realised.

ground, filtering laboriously through the fissures and clefts of the rocks until it illuminates the group in the foreground, with its rigorously pyramidal structure.

Leonardo da Vinci (1452-1519)
Mona Lisa (or The Gioconda)

Reams have been written about this small masterpiece by Leonardo, and the gentle woman who is its subject has been adapted in turn as an aesthetic, philosophical and advertising symbol, entering eventually into the irreverent parodies of the Dada and Surrealist artists. The history of the panel has been much discussed, although it remains in part uncertain. According to Vasari, the subject is a young Florentine woman, Monna (or Mona) Lisa, who in 1495 married the well-known figure, Francesco del Giocondo, and thus came to be known as "La Gioconda". The work should probably be dated during Leonardo's second Florentine period, that is between 1503 and 1505. Leonardo himself loved the portrait, so much so that he always carried it with him until eventually in France it was sold to Francis I, either by Leonardo or by Melzi. From the beginning it was greatly admired and much copied, and it came to be considered the prototype of the Renaissance portrait. It became even more famous in 1911, when it was stolen from the Salon Carré in the Louvre, being rediscovered in a hotel in Florence two years later. It is difficult to discuss such a work briefly because of the complex stylistic motifs which are part of it. In the essay " On the perfect beauty of a woman ", by the 16th-century writer Firenzuola, we learn that the slight opening of the lips at the corners of the mouth was considered in that period a sign of elegance. Thus Mona Lisa has that slight smile which enters into the gentle, delicate atmosphere pervading the whole painting. To achieve this effect, Leonardo uses the *sfumato* technique, a gradual dissolving of the forms themselves, continuous interaction between light and shade and an uncertain sense of the time of day.

Leonardo da Vinci (1452-1519)
The Virgin of the Rocks

Begun, according to some critics, in Florence in 1483 but not completed until about 1490, this magnificent work corresponds to another version (most of which was painted by Ambrogio de Predis), now in the National Gallery in London. Leonardo may have received the commission for the work from the Confraternity of San Francesco Grande in Milan; certainly, at any rate, the painting was at Fontainebleau in 1625, and this may permit us to deduce that it was part of the group of works by Leonardo acquired by Francis I. The light in this painting comes from the back-

PLACE VENDÔME

Another masterpiece by Jules Hardouin-Mansart (who had already designed Place des Victoires), this square received its name from from the fact that the Duke of Vendôme had his residence here. It was created between 1687 and 1720 to surround an equestrian statue by Girardon dedicated to Louis XIV, later destroyed, like so many others, during the Revolution. A perfect example of stylistic simplicity and austerity, it is octagonal in form and surrounded by buildings which have large arches on the lower floor; on the foreparts of the buildings are skilfully distributed pediments and they are crowned, on the roofs, by numerous dormer-windows, so typical that some have thought to see in this square a synthesis of the spirit and style of Paris. There are important buildings here today: the famous Hôtel Ritz at number 15, the house where Chopin died in 1849 at number 12 and the residence of Eugenia de Montijo, future wife of Napoleon III. In the centre of the square stands the famous column erected by Gondouin and Lepère between 1806 and 1810 in honour of Napoleon I. Inspired by the Column of Trajan in Rome, it is 145 feet high and around the shaft is a spiral series of bas-reliefs, cast from the 1200 canons captured at Austerlitz, in which the sculptor Bergeret sought to hand down to posterity the Napoleonic exploits. On the top of the column, Antoine-Denise Chaudet erected a statue of the emperor which was destroyed in 1814 and replaced by that of Henry IV. Later, in 1863, a statue of Napoleon was put back in place, but eight years later again, at the time of the Commune (when the voice of the great painter Gustave Courbet had a decisive say), the statue was taken down once more, only to be replaced once and for all by another replica of Napoleon three years afterwards.

OPÉRA

The largest theatre for lyric opera in the world (in fact its surface area covers nearly 120,000 square feet, it can accommodate more than 2000 people and there is room on its stage for no less than 450 performers), it is also perhaps the most interesting building from the era of Napoleon III. Designed by Garnier and built between 1862 and 1875, its façade displays that profusion of decorative elements which was typical of the era. An ample stairway leads up to the first of the two orders into which the façade is divided, with its large arches and robust pillars, in front of which are numerous marble groups of sculpture. At the second pillar on the right can be seen what is considered the masterpiece of Jean-Baptiste Carpeaux, "The Dance" (the original is now in the Louvre). The second order of the façade consists of tall double columns which frame large windows; above is an attic, with exuberant decoration, and above this again the flattened cupola. The interior is just as highly decorated as the façade: the monumental stairway is enriched by marbles, the vault is decorated with paintings by Isidore Pils and the hall has a large painting by Chagall done in 1966.

LA MADELEINE

A Greek temple in the middle of Paris, this is certainly a rather extraordinary structure. It was Napoleon who wanted to erect a monument in honour of the Great Army, built along the lines of the Maison Carrée at Nîmes. To do so, he had a previous structure, which was not yet complete, totally demolished, and work was resumed from scratch in 1806, under the direction of the architect Vignon. In 1814 it became a church dedicated to St. Mary Magdalene, standing in the centre of the square of the same name. It has the form and structure of a classical Greek temple: a high base with a large stairway in front, a colonnade with with 52 Corinthian columns 65 feet high running round the outside of the structure and a pediment with a large frieze sculpted by Lemaire in 1834 and representing the Last Judgment. The interior is aisleless, and it has a vestibule, in which are two sculptural groups by Pradier and Rude, and a semicircular apse. Above the high altar is a work by an Italian artist, the Assumption of Mary Magdalene by Marocchetti. As one leaves the building, one's gaze takes in the whole length of the Rue Royale, as far as the obelisk in Place de la Concorde and the Palais Bourbon.

PONT ALEXANDRE III

One of Paris's many bridges, this has a single metal span 350 feet long and 130 feet wide joining the Esplanade des Invalides to the Champs-Elysées. Built between 1896 and 1900, it is named after the czar Alexander III whose son, Nicholas II, performed its inauguration. In fact the bridge was built to celebrate the creation of the alliance between the Russians and the French. Garlands of flowers, lamps held up by cherubs and allegorical figures of marine deities make up the decorative motifs of the bridge. On the two pilons on the right bank are representations of medieval France and modern France, while on the left-bank pilons are statues representing Renaissance France and the France of the time of Louis XIV. Allegorical representations of the Seine and the Neva, symbols again of France and Russia, decorate the pilons at the entries to the bridge.

CARROUSEL ARCH

Designed by Pierre-François Fontaine and Charles Percier and built between 1806 and 1808, it celebrates the victories of Napoleon Bonaparte in 1805. It could be said to be an imitation of the Arch of Septimius Severus in Rome, repeating as it does that monument's architecture and plastic decoration. Red and white marble columns frame the three vaults and each front is filled with bas-reliefs which recall the Emperor's victories. On top of it were placed the four gilded horses which were removed by order of Napoleon from the Venetian basilica of S. Marco, to which they were returned in 1815. The originals were then replaced with copies, to which a chariot and the statue of Peace were later added.

THE GARDEN OF THE TUILERIES

It stretches about one kilometre from Place du Carrousel to Place de la Concorde. The ground was bought by Catherine de' Medici in 1563 to create an English style garden. Embellished by Le Nôtre in 1663, the present garden of the Tuileries consists of two large areas connected by a central avenue flanked by flower-beds containing statues.

PLACE DE LA CONCORDE

Created between 1757 and 1779 to a design by Jacques-Ange Gabriel on land donated by the king in 1743, the square was originally dedicated to Louis XV and there was an equestrian statue of the king, a work by Bouchardon and Pigalle, in the centre, pulled down during the French Revolution. In the Revolution, this became the site of the guillotine, under whose blade so many great figures of the time lost their heads: from the king, Louis XVI, and his queen, Marie Antoinette, to Madame Roland and Robespierre. The square became Place de la Concorde in 1795, and its present-day appearance dates from work supervised by the architect Hittorf between 1836 and 1840. In the centre of the square today stands the Egyptian obelisk from the temple of Luxor, donated to Louis Philippe in 1831 by Mehmet-Ali. Erected in 1836, it is 75 feet high and covered with hieroglyphics which illustrate the glorious deeds of the pharaoh

Ramses II. Eight statues, symbolising the main cities of France, stand at the corners of the square. To the north of the square, on either side of Rue Royale, are the colonnaded buildings (these too designed by Gabriel) containing the Ministry of the Navy and the Hôtel Crillon.

PLACE DE LA CONCORDE
Fountain

Built on the model of the fountains in Piazza S. Pietro in Rome, these two fountains at the sides of the obelisk were erected by Hittorf between 1836 and 1846; they have several basins and the statues adorning them represent fluvial allegories. There are perhaps few squares in the world with the magic atmosphere of enchantment present at every hour of the day in this square. Indeed at night, under the light of the street-lamps, its atmosphere becomes unreal, almost fable-like.

GRAND PALAIS

The World Fair held in Paris in 1900 was an important step in the history of the city's art and architecture. For the occasion, monuments and works of art were created in a modern style which was almost too eclectic and bombastic. As a reflection of this taste, the two adjacent buildings called the Petit Palais and the Grand Palais were erected, both of huge dimensions and characterised by their ample colonnades, friezes and sculptural compositions. The Grand Palais, built by Deglane and Louvet, has a façade with Ionic columns, 787 feet long and 65 feet high. Today important artistic events take place here, including exhibitions of painting, whereas previously its vast area served for fairs, motor shows and similar exhibitions. Part of it is permanently occupied by the Palais de la Découverte (Discovery), where the latest conquests of science and steps in man's progress are celebrated.

GRAND PALAIS - Chariot

The corners of the Grand Palais are crowned by enormous chariots, like the one shown here, which give very much the impression that they want to hurl themselves from the points where they stand into the surrounding space. The inside of the Grand Palais has a huge room covered by a flattened cupola 141 feet high.

PETIT PALAIS

Built by Charles Girault for the World Fair in 1900 in an eclectic style typical of the late 19th century, it consists of a monumental portico crowned by a dome and flanked by two colonnades. At present, it contains the collection of the City of Paris formed by countless 19th century paintings and sculptures (Géricault, Delacroix, Courbet, Redon, etc.); it is, therefore, an interesting stopover between the Louvre and the Orsay Museum. Furthermore, it houses the Tuck and Dutuit collections which not only feature ancient Greek, Roman and Egyptian objects but also drawings and paintings from different periods and places (Dürer, Cranach, Watteau, Guardi, etc.).

ORSAY MUSEUM

What the press defined as "the most beautiful museum in Europe" is to be found on the left bank of the Seine, where the State Audit Court originally stood in 1870; it was then destroyed during the Commune. In 1898 the Paris-Orléans railway company assigned the building of the new station to Victor Laloux. The work was carried out in two years so that the Gare d'Orsay was ready for the universal exhibition held in 1900. Laloux designed a grandiose nave 135 metres by 40 metres, the metal structure of which was skilfully covered on the outside by light coloured stuccowork. The interior not only housed the sixteen platforms but also restaurants and an elegant hotel with at least 400 rooms. Abandoned in 1939, the Gare d'Orsay went on a slow decline under the spectre of demolition: Orson Welles's cultural revival with the filming of *The Trial* or the establishment of Jean-Louis Barrault's company there were of no avail. In 1973 the French President at the time, Georges Pompidou, declared it a national monument and saw to it that a museum displaying the half century of art that goes from Napoleon III's Second Empire to the beginnings of Cubism was up there. It proved to be a perfect link between the Louvre, a temple of ancient art, and the Centre Georges Pompidou, a temple of modern art. The tender for contract for its restructuring commenced in 1978 and was won by the ACT group; the Italian architect, Mrs. Gae Aulenti, was entrusted with the interior decorating. Nowadays more than 4,000 works including paintings, sculptures, drawings and furniture are exhibited in over 45,000 square metres.

The **ground floor** features paintings, sculptures and decorative arts from 1850 to 1870, with works by Ingres, Delacroix, Manet, Puvis de Chavannes and Gustave Moreau whereas Impressionist paintings (Monet, Renoir, Pissarro, Degas and Manet), Personnaz, Gachet and Guillaumin collections and Post-Impressionist paintings with masterpieces by Seurat, Signac, Toulouse-Lautrec, Gauguin, Van Gogh and the Nabis group (Bonnard, Vuillard and Vallotton) are displayed on the **top floor.** Lastly, the **middle floor** features art from 1870 to 1914, with the official art of the III Republic, Symbolism, academic painting and the decorative arts of the Art Nouveau period, with Guimard, Emile Gallé and the School of Nancy.

CHAMPS-ÉLYSÉES

Originally this vast area lying to the west of Place de la Concorde was swamp land. After its reclamation, le Nôtre in 1667 designed the wide avenue called Grand-Cours (it became the Champs-Elysées in 1709), reaching from the Tuileries as far as Place dell'Etoile, today called Place de Gaulle. At the beginning of the avenue are the horses of Marly, a work by Guillaume Coustou; from this point as far as the Ronde Point of the Champs-Elysées the avenue is flanked by a park. At the time of the Second Empire, this became the most fashionable meeting-place and upper-class residential area in all Paris. Today it may no longer have its one-time aristocratic character, but it has lost nothing of its beauty and elegance: luxurious shops, theatres, famous restaurants and important airline offices line its wide footpaths, which are always full of Parisians, tourists and a cosmopolitan throng.

ARCH OF TRIUMPH

At the end of the Champs-Elysées, at the top of the Chaillot hill, is the large Place de Gaulle; radiating outwards from this square are no less than twelve main arteries. Isolated in the centre stands the powerful and imposing Arch of Triumph, begun by Chalgrin in 1806 under Napoleon, who ordered it as a memorial to the Great Army. Completed in 1836, it has a single barrel-vault and actually exceeds in size the Arch of Constantine in Rome: in fact it is 164 feet high and 147 feet wide. The faces of the arch have huge bas-reliefs, of which the best known and finest piece is that on the right, on the part of the arch facing the Champs-Elysées, depicting the departure of the volunteers in 1792 and called the " Marseillaise ". The principal victories of Napoleon are celebrated in the other bas-reliefs higher up, while the shields sculpted in the top section bear the names of the great battles. Under the arch the Tomb of the Unknown Soldier was placed in 1920 and its eternal flame is tended every evening. There is a history of the monument in a small museum inside the arch, where one can read the names of no less than 558 generals, some of them underlined because they died on the battlefield.

EIFFEL TOWER

If the symbol of Rome is the Colosseum, then Paris's symbol is without doubt the Eiffel Tower: both are monuments unique in planning and construction, both stir admiration by their extraordinary dimensions, and both bear witness to man's inborn will to build something capable of demonstrating the measure of his genius. The tower was erected on the occasion of the World Fair in 1889. These were the years of the Industrial Revolution, of progress and of scientific conquests. The attempt was made to adapt every art to the new direction which life had taken and to make every human activity correspond to the new sensibility created by the rapidly changing times. Architecture also underwent radical changes: glass, iron and steel were the new construction materials, the most suitable ones to make buildings lighter, more dynamic and more modern. The engineer, in short, had taken the place of the architect. And indeed it was an engineer, Gustave Eiffel, who designed — not on paper but on the surface of the sky itself — these extraordinary lines of metal, which soar above the Parisian skyline and seem to triumph over all the older monuments of the city. While the older buildings symbolise the past, the Eiffel Tower anticipates the future and the conquests which man will achieve.

Altogether 1050 feet high, the Eiffel Tower is an extremely light, interlaced structure in which no less than 15,000 pieces of metal are welded together. Its extraordinary weight of 7000 tons rests on four enormous pilons with cement bases. It has three floors: the first at 187 feet, the second at 377 feet and the third at 899 feet. On each of the floors there are bars and restaurants, allowing the tourist to pause there and enjoy the unique panoramic view: at times, on days when the visibility is perfect, one can see almost 45 miles. Beneath the Eiffel Tower is the green area of the Champs-de-Mars, a military field at one time but later transformed into a garden. During the Ancien Régime and during the Revolution many festivals were held here, including the Festival of the Supreme Being, introduced by Robespierre and celebrated on 8 June 1794. Then, in modern times, the vast area has been used for numerous World Fairs. Today the garden, whose design was supervised by Formigé between 1908 and 1928, is divided by wide avenues and scattered with flower gardens and small watercourses.

PALAIS DE CHAILLOT

Another World Fair, the one held in 1937, was the occasion for which this building was constructed. It was designed by the architects Boileau, Carlu and Azéma on the site of a previous building, the Trocadéro. The Palais de Chaillot has a central terrace with statues of gilded bronze, uniting two enormous pavilions which stretch out into two wings, as if in a long, curving embrace. From here a splendid complex of terraces, stairways and gardens slopes down to the Seine, a triumph of greenery made even more pleasant by the sounds of waterfalls and the jets of fountains. The two pavilions, on the front of which are inscribed verses by the poet Valéry, today contain the Museum of French Monuments (an important collection of medieval works), the Museum of the Navy (in which is a model of the ship " La Belle Poule " which brought back Napoleon's remains from St. Helena) and the Museum of Man, with its wealth of anthropological collections and documentation of the human race.

MILITARY SCHOOL

This building, which stands at the south end of the Champs-de-Mars, was constructed as a result of the initiative of the financier Pâris-Duverney and of Madame Pompadour, both of whom wanted young men of the poorer classes to be able to take up military careers. Jacques-Ange Gabriel was the architect of the building, erected between 1751 and 1773 in a sober style characterised by its harmonious lines. The façade has two orders of windows, and in the centre is a pavilion with columns which support the pediment, decorated with statues and covered by a cupola. On the back, from Place de Fontenoy, one can see the elegant Courtyard of Honour with its portico of twin Doric columns and a façade formed by three pavilions linked by two rows of columns. The building still serves as a military school today. In 1784 Napoleon Bonaparte entered it as a pupil, to leave the following year with the rank of second lieutenant in the artillery.

LES INVALIDES

Stretching between Place Vauban and the Esplanade des Invalides, this vast complex of buildings includes the Hôtel des Invalides, the Dôme and the church of St. Louis. The whole construction, ordered by Louis XIV and entrusted to

Libéral Bruant in 1671, was designed as a refuge for old and invalid soldiers who were then often forced to beg for a living. Completed in 1676, it later saw the addition of the church of St. Louis and the Dôme, designed by J. Harduoin-Mansart. The vast square of the Esplanade, 520 yards long and 270 yards wide, designed between 1704 and 1720, creates the right surroundings for the Hôtel des Invalides. In the garden in front of the Hôtel are a line of bronze cannon from the 17th and 18th centuries, eighteen pieces which belong to the " triumphal battery " and are fired only on important occasions, and at the sides of the entrance are two German tanks captured in 1944. The severe and dignified façade, 643 feet long, has four orders of windows and a majestic portal in the centre, surmounted by a relief representing Louis XIV with Prudence and Justice at his sides. Entering the courtyard, one can see the regular forms of the four sides with their two storeys of arcades. The pavilion at the end thus becomes the façade of the church of St. Louis. In the centre is the statue of Napoleon by Seurre, which was previously on top of the column in Place Vendôme. Worth seeing inside the church of St. Louis-des-Invalides is the Chapel of Napoleon, in which is kept the hearse in which the remains of the emperor were taken to St. Helena for burial and the sarcophagus in which Napoleon's body was brought back to France in 1840.

on the following page

DÔME DES INVALIDES

Considered one of the masterpieces of the architect Hardouin-Mansart, it was erected between 1679 and 1706. Pure forms and a classical, sober style are the characteristics of this building, with its square plan and two orders. The façade

is a work of elegance and symmetry: above the two orders of columns surmounted by a pediment is the solid mass of the drum with its twin columns, from which, after a sober series of corbels, the slim cupola springs with its decorations of flower garlands and other floral motifs. The gilded leaves with which the top is decorated shine in the sunlight, and the structure is terminated by a small lantern with spire 350 feet above ground level. The interior, in the form of a Greek cross, reflects the simplicity characteristic of the exterior. In the pendentives of the dome Charles de la Fosse painted the four Evangelists, while in the centre he depicted the figure of St. Louis offering Christ the sword with which he has defeated the infidels. Directly under the dome is the entrance to the crypt which contains the tomb of Napoleon. Indeed, this church could be said to be a shrine to the memory of Napoleon. Here too are tombs of members of the emperor's family, as well as those of other great Frenchmen. In the chapels on the right are the tombs of Napoleon's brother, Joseph Bonaparte, and of the two marshals Vauban and Foch. The emperor's other brother, Jérôme, is buried in the first chapel on the left, and his tomb is followed by those of Turenne and Lyautey.

TOMB OF NAPOLEON I

Napoleon Bonaparte died on 5 May 1821 on St. Helena, but not until seven years later were the French able to obtain permission from England to bring back the remains of their emperor to his own country. Louis Philippe sent his son, the prince of Joinville, to St. Helena to supervise the exhumation of the emperor's body. The re-entry into France was the last triumphal voyage of the Frenchman best loved by his people, most venerated by his soldiers and most feared by his enemies. In September 1840 a French ship carried the body of Napoleon to Le Havre, then slowly made the entire trip up the Seine as far as Paris. On 15 September, in a snow storm, almost the entire city attended the funeral of the emperor, whose body moved in a slow procession along the great boulevards, passing under the Arch of Triumph and descending the Champs-Elysées to come to rest here in the Dôme des Invalides and thus end at last Napoleon's long exile. Like those of an Egyptian pharaoh, the remains were contained in six coffins: the first of tin, the second of mahogany, the third and fourth of lead, the fifth of ebony and the sixth of oak. These were then placed in the huge sarcophagus of red granite, in the crypt specially planned for the purpose by the great architect Visconti. Here

12 enormous Victories, the work of Pradier, keep a vigil over the emperor, as if to symbolise the whole French people, finally reunited with their great hero. And is if to unite him after death with one from whom he had been divided during his life, next to the tomb was placed the tomb of Napoleon's son, the King of Rome, known romantically as l'Aiglon (the " Eaglet ").

PALAIS DU LUXEMBOURG

On the death of Henry IV, his queen, Maria de' Medici, who apparently did not feel at home in the Louvre, preferred to live in a place which in some way reminded her of Florence, the city from which she came. Thus in 1612 she acquired this mansion from the duke François de Luxembourg, together with a considerable expanse of ground, and in 1615 she commissioned Salomon de Brosse to build a palace as near as possible in style and materials to the Florentine palaces which she had left to come to France. And in fact both the rusticated stonework and the large columns and rings are much more reminiscent of the Palazzo Pitti in Florence that of any other Parisian building. The façade consists of a pavilion with two orders covered by a cupola and with two pavilions at the sides, united to the central unit by galleries. When the Revolution broke out, the palace was taken from the royal family and transformed into a state prison.

ST. ETIENNE DU MONT

This church, one of the most remarkable in Paris both for its façade and for the interior, stands in the city's most picturesque zone, the Latin Quarter. From as early as the 13th century the University of Paris was established here, a university which immediately became famous throughout the world of Western culture because of the names of the great masters who gave lessons there: St. Bonaventura and St. Thomas Aquinas, to name only the most important. In this area, then, the original St. Etienne du Mont was built; it was begun in 1492 but completed only in 1622 with the construction of the façade. It is impossible not to be struck by the originality of this church. In fact, the façade is a bizarre amalgamation of the Gothic and Renaissance styles, but its three superimposed pediments, because of their very peculiarity, succeed in creating a unified and coherent appearance. The church also contains the reliquary of the patron saint of Paris, St. Geneviève, who in 451 saved the city from the threat of the Huns.

Interior

If the façade of the church is surprising because of its composite appearance, the interior is equally so because of the architectural innovations it contains. In Gothic style with three aisles and transept, the interior has very high cylindrical piers which support the vaults and are linked together by a gallery above the arches. But the most picturesque part of the interior of the church, which makes St. Etienne unique of its kind in Paris, is the " jubé ", that is, the suspended gallery which separates the nave from the choir. Possibly designed by Philibert Delorme, it is the only " jubé " known in Paris and its construction dates from between 1521 and about 1545.

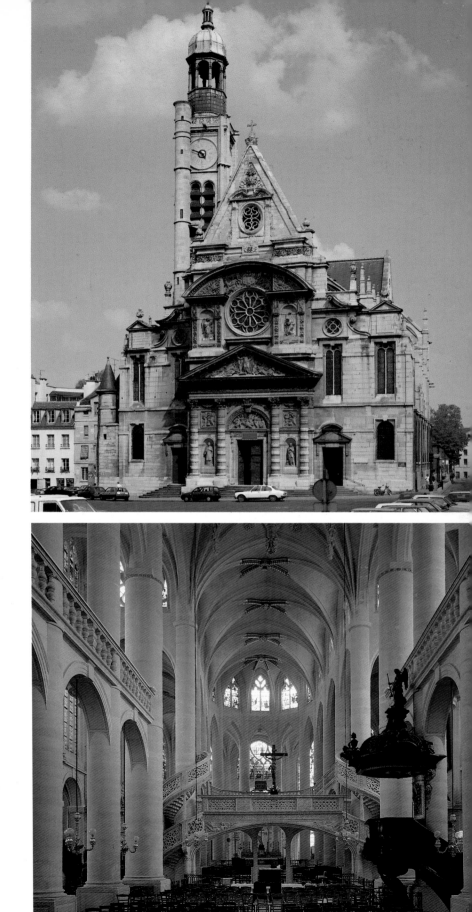

ST -GERMAIN-DES-PRÉS

Here one is emerged once more in the animated life of the quarter of St. Germain, whose typical and colourful streets interweave and cross one another to form picturesque corners. Here too is the church of Sainte-Germain-des-Prés, the oldest church in Paris, built between the 11th and 12th centuries, and destroyed no less than four times in forty years by the Normans, but each time rebuilt in its severe Romanesque forms. In the façade one can see the remains of the 12th-century portal, unfortunately half-hidden by the 17th-century portico erected in 1607. The bell-tower, on the other hand, is entirely Romanesque, its corners reinforced and thickened by robust buttresses. In the 19th century, the two towers which stood at the sides of the choir were demolished, and of the choir itself there are only a few remains. The interior has three aisles and a transept, the end of which was modified in the 17th century. As a result of the restoration of the church in the 19th century, the vaults and capitals now have decorations too rich to allow the otherwise simple and severe structure of the interior fully to be appreciated. The most interesting part of the building is the choir with its ambulatory, where the original architecture of the 12th century is still in part preserved intact. In this church are the tombs of two illustrious figures: that of Cartesius, in the second chapel on the right, and that of the Polish king John Casimir, in the transept on the left.

PANTHÉON

Born as the church of Sainte Geneviève in fulfilment of a vow made by Louis XV during a serious illness in 1744, it was designed by Soufflot, begun in 1758 and completed with the contribution of Rondelet in 1789. During the Revolution it became the Temple of Glory, used for the burial of great men; under Napoleon it was reopened for worship in 1806, but only until 1885, when it returned once and for all to its status as a secular temple. Soufflot, in designing it, sought a decidedly classical style, returning to the ancient world. Its dimensions, first of all, are exceptional: 360 feet long by 272 feet high. A stairway in front of the temple leads up to a pronaos with 22 columns, which support a pediment on which in 1831 David d'Angers sculpted the allegorical work representing the Fatherland between Liberty and History. Here one can also read the famous inscription: " Aux grandes hommes, la patrie reconnaisante " (" To the great men, from their grateful fatherland "). The whole building is dominated by the great cupola, similar to Christopher Wren's dome on the church of St. Paul in London; here too, the drum is surrounded by a ring of Corinthian columns. The interior is in the form of a Greek cross, with the cupola above the crossing, supported by four piers, on one of which is the tomb of Rousseau. The walls are decorated with paintings, of which the most famous are those by Puvis de Chavannes, illustrating stories of St. Geneviève. The crypt which lies below the temple contains many tombs of illustrious men. Worth recalling are those of Victor Hugo (brought here in 1885), Emile Zola, Voltaire, the designer Soufflot himself, Carnot and Mirabeau. There are 425 steps leading up to the top of the cupola, from which there is a vast and impressive panorama.

MOULIN-ROUGE

Like Montparnasse, but even more so, Montmartre was and still is one of the most curious and picturesque quarters of Paris. It stands on a limestone hill 425 feet high where, according to the legend, St. Denis, the first bishop of Paris, was decapitated in 272. Some believe that the area's name derives from this fact: originally called " mons Martyrum " (Mount of the Martyrs), it later acquired its present form. Throughout the 19th century, this was the mecca of all those artists who believed that the Bohemian life meant living freely, making one's art the main reason for living and rejecting any attempt from without to impose a way of life. Every painter, from the most famous to the most humble, has left a trace of his life and art at Montmartre. At the foot of the hill (the " butte Montmartre "), is Place Blanche, dominated by the long blades of the windmill of the Moulin Rouge (" Red Windmill "), founded in 1889, where the artists Valentin le Désossé, Jane Avril and La Goulue performed. This cabaret, on whose stage the " can-can " was born, is linked to the memory of the painter Toulouse-Lautrec, who passed his nights here setting down with his brush the most curious and picturesque details and the truest and most humane images of the night life of the cabarets and theatres. Here those personages who lived for art, but were excluded from the art blessed by official recognition, finally found their place. Depicted on a grand scale in the posters of Toulouse-Lautrec, they achieved a renown which they had never had on the boards of the Moulin-Rouge.

THE OPÉRA BASTILLE

Designed by the Canadian architect, Carlos Ott, who won the international competition launched in 1982 for the construction of an "opera theater for the people" on the site that is synonynous with the French Revolution, the Opéra Bastille was inaugurated on July 14, 1989.

The complex, which includes various modern facilities, is characterized in particular by a monumental semicylinder in glass which encloses a large hall with a seating capacity of 2,700. The building respects the surroundings and opens onto the square with an arch that is aligned with the adjacent houses.

PLACE DE LA REPUBLIQUE

This vast rectangular plaza was created by Haussmann (1854) as an area for the maneuvers of the troops sent to put down the popular uprisings. At the center stands the monument with the statue of the Republic (1883), set on a pedestal decorated with bronze bas-reliefs by Dalou which depict events in the history of the Republic.

PLACE
DU TERTRE

The concept of painting which was current in former times — that of the painter who lived as a painter and lived only for his painting — has changed today, but this is perhaps not true of at least one place: Place du Tertre. Not that time has stopped here: the process of change has gone on, introducing all those new personalities and new things which are an inevitable part of modern times. It would be foolish to come to Place du Tertre and the tiny streets around it looking for traces of the atmosphere of the good old days: here, as everywhere, the alterations brought by time have

had their inexorable effect on man and his surroundings.

SACRÉ-CŒUR

From whatever part of the city one surveys the panorama of Paris, one's eye finally comes to rest on the white domes of Sacré-Cœur. Standing majestically on the top of the hill of Montmartre, it was erected in 1876 by national subscription and consecrated in 1919. Its architects (among the most important were Abadie and Magno) designed it in a curious style which is a mixture of Romanesque and Byzantine. The four small domes and the large central dome, standing solidly on the high drum, are typically Oriental. On the back part, a square bell-tower 275 feet high

contains the famous " Savoyarde ", a bell weighing no less than 19 tons and thus one of the biggest in the world. Dignified steps lead up to the façade of the church and the porch with three arches which stands in front of it; above are equestrian statues of what are perhaps the two historical figures best loved by the French, King Louis the Blessed and Joan of Arc. The interior, because of its decorations of reliefs, paintings and mosaics which in places are incredibly elaborate, can almost be said to have lost its architectural consistency. From the inside of the church, one can descend into the vast underground crypt, or else climb up to the top of the cupola, from which there is a panoramic view of the city and its surrounding areas extending for miles.

CONTENTS